Spark

Poetry and Art Inspired by the Novels of Muriel Spark

edited by Rob A. Mackenzie
and Louise Peterkin

Blue Diode Press
Edinburgh

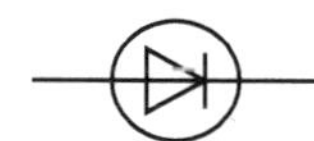

First published in 2018 by Blue Diode Press
30 Lochend Road
Leith
Edinburgh EH6 8BS
www.bluediode.co.uk

ISBN: 978-1-9164051-0-3

Typesetting: Rob A. Mackenzie.
text in Minion Pro, 11 pt; headers and footers in Myriad Pro.

Cover design and typography: Gerry Cambridge.
Cover image of Latin inscription: Jeroen Fortgens/Shutterstock.
Diode logo design: Sam and Ian Alexander.

Printed and bound by Imprint Digital, Exeter, UK.
https://digital.imprint.co.uk

CONTENTS

Foreword
Introduction
Spiritus Sanctus

THE COMFORTERS (1957)
W.N. Herbert The Muriels 11
Polly Atkin Paper Pellets on a Saucer 13

ROBINSON (1958)
Judy Brown Waiting for the Pomegranate Boat 15
Matthew Francis Island 16

MEMENTO MORI (1959)
Sean O'Brien Memento Mori 17
Helena Nelson Mrs Pettigrew Replies 19

THE BALLAD OF PECKHAM RYE (1960)
Sasha Dugdale A Deformed Ballad 20
Drew Milne The Ballad of Peckham Rye 23

THE BACHELORS (1960)
Jeanette Lynes Vocations 26
Paul Batchelor Cold Reading 27

Lisa Smithey ***'untitled'*** 29

THE PRIME OF MISS JEAN BRODIE (1961)
Tishani Doshi Face Exercises for Marionette Lines 30
Vahni Capildeo Futurist Cleopatra 32

THE GIRLS OF SLENDER MEANS (1963)
Richard Price Girl of Slender Means 35
Lindsey Shields Waters 7" by 14" – a Casement Study 36

THE MANDELBAUM GATE (1965)
Robert Alan Jamieson Partition 38
M.G. Garland Same Hell Anyway 41

THE PUBLIC IMAGE (1968)
Andy Jackson Lady Tiger 43
Rishi Dastidar A Man of Theory on the Via Publica 45

Rachael Macarthur ***'Slo-mo song'*** 47

THE DRIVER'S SEAT (1970)
Tessa Berring Don't Buy Slippers Buy a Little Knife 48
Deborah Alma I will not tell you anything you want to hear 50

NOT TO DISTURB (1971)
Iain Matheson Disturb 51
Larry Butler [NOT TO DISTURB] 52

THE HOTHOUSE BY THE EAST RIVER (1971)
James Sheard Tulpas 54
Janette Ayachi Elsa's Shadow Falls Toward the Sun 56

THE ABBESS OF CREWE (1974)
Simon Barraclough Divine Hours 59
Sarah Bernstein The Hour of None 61

THE TAKEOVER (1976)
Iain Morrison Despoiler Alert 63
Zoë Brigley Letter from Nemi 72

TERRITORIAL RIGHTS (1978)
Colin Herd Two sweaters for one person or one sweater for more than one 74
Eileen Pun Studio Apartment: Eyrie 75

LOITERING WITH INTENT (1981)
Anna Selby Sea Flower 77
Joanne Limburg The Benediction of St Muriel 78

Natalie Gale* *'untitled' 79

THE ONLY PROBLEM (1984)
Juana Adcock Clara, Jemima and Eye-Paint 80
Tony Williams The Book of Harvey 83

A FAR CRY FROM KENSINGTON (1988)
Lisa Kelly Pisseur de Copie 85
Jane Bonnyman The Box 88

SYMPOSIUM (1990)
Frances Leviston The Last Word 90
Rob A. Mackenzie *Les Autres* 91

REALITY AND DREAMS (1996)
Gerry Loose Reality and Dreams 93
Louise Peterkin Sister Agnieszka *Is* Carmine Revenge 95

AIDING AND ABETTING (2000)
Tim Turnbull An Evil Twin 97
Lily Blacksell I want you to know I believe in myself 98

THE FINISHING SCHOOL (2004)
Dzifa Benson Comme il Faut 100
Matthew Caley The Fern 102

Nazia Mohammad* *'here' 104

Notes 105
Acknowledgements 106
Biographies 107

Editors' Foreword

Rob A. Mackenzie & Louise Peterkin

When we first thought about asking poets to respond to the work of Muriel Spark, our plans were modest: a small pamphlet, a handful of poems inspired by her most popular novels. But, soon, we decided to add a few works of modernist art responding either to particular Spark novels or to her work in general. We liked many of the lesser-known novels and wanted to include a wide variety of poets. Two poets to each book, we thought, might be interesting. How would two very different writers deal with the same book?

We are delighted with the result. We asked poets already considered to be among the best of their generation and some who aren't as well known (yet) as they ought to be. We've created this anthology in the belief that they matter. A good poem offers more depth, restorative energy and emotional intelligence than the slogans, screens and 'truths' we are bombarded with every day. Poems, however, need to be read and often re-read before they work their magic. We believe it's worth doing.

W.N. Herbert will guide you through many Muriels; Robert Alan Jamieson ruminates on religious and political tension in Jerusalem; Lisa Kelly wittily channels a "pisseur de copie"; Dzifa Benson arranges flowers that aren't there. Every poem ought to be a surprise, and we hope that is continually true of this book.

September, 2018

Introduction

Olga Wojtas

The centenary celebrations of Muriel Spark's birth in 1918 are particularly valuable in making her better known for more than just the book she called her "milch cow," *The Prime of Miss Jean Brodie*.

Muriel Spark wrote another twenty-one novels, and was also a short story writer, an essayist, a reviewer – and a poet. As a primary pupil at James Gillespie's High School for Girls, she went to Morningside Library at least twice a week. In her autobiography, *Curriculum Vitae*, she writes: "I would bring home four books at a time, most of them poetry, for I was destined to poetry by all my mentors."

Her favourite poets included Wordsworth, Browning, Tennyson, Rupert Brooke, Walter de la Mare and John Masefield. And she loved the Border ballads, reading them so often that she memorised them. "The steel and bite of the ballads, so remorseless and yet so lyrical, entered my literary bloodstream, never to depart."

She enjoyed "a certain fame as the school's poet," with five poems published in an anthology, *The Door of Youth*, when she was twelve. She had poems published in the school magazine, and won an external competition with a poem on Sir Walter Scott. The adjudicator was the Edinburgh poet Lewis Spence, a former editor of *The Scotsman*, who told her: "Of course you will write as a profession."

Aged twenty-nine, she became general secretary of the Poetry Society and editor of its journal, the *Poetry Review.* When she embarked on writing a novel in 1954, it was with the conviction that formally, the novel as an art form was essentially a type of poem.

"I was convinced that any good novel, or indeed any composition which called for a constructional sense, was essentially an extension of poetry."

She won a competition with the very first short story she wrote, *The Seraph and the Zambesi.* When the tax authorities attempted to take a cut of the prize money, she responded tartly: "I am not a short story writer. The only *creative* writing I do is poetry."

And in her autobiography, she states: "I always tell students of my work, and interviewers, that I think of myself as predominantly a poet." The slab marking her grave in Italy is inscribed with the simple word *Poeta.*

In this new anthology, poets are given the chance to respond to Spark's novels. She would surely approve of this symbiosis, and be delighted by the fine work her own has evoked.

i. m. Matthew Sweeney (1952–2018)
who would have been in this anthology
had health and time allowed

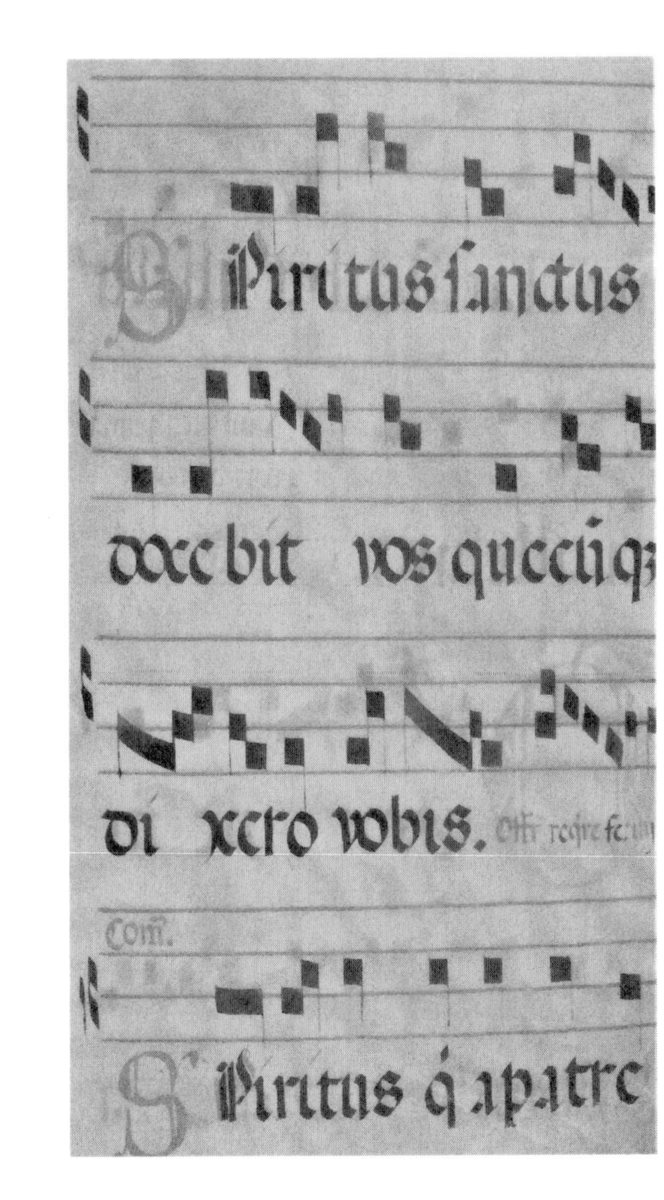

Spiritus sanctus
docebit vos quecũq
dixero vobis.
Com.
Spiritus q a patre

W.N. Herbert

The Muriels

Muriel made a note to call Muriel to look after the cats
while she was visiting Muriel in Monifieth. Muriel could tell
the other Muriels she wouldn't make their monthly meeting.

The Six Muriels they had called them at school, or rather
Miss McClennan had, for she had been a Muriel too, as well
as their history teacher, and was alluding to the original six,

maidservants to the much-pestered Muriel, Queen of Scots.
They had always been on hand, as it were, to thrust an arm through
the door-staples in castle after castle, or so it seemed,

thinking back to the inefficient viciousnesses of the past.
She made a note to get the oven cleaned on her return.
How she had come to know the further, farther away Muriels

she couldn't always recall – it wasn't as though she had sought
them out, or that there was a network of Muriels, passing on
their details, or gathering in certain known tearooms –

except, in a sense, thanks to coincidence, or fate, call it
what you will, now there was. She put the pencil down, but
its scratching continued. Thinking how her handwriting

aged her, she ran through her list of all the Muriels.
It comforted her, like a prayer, as indeed did the company
of Muriels. It wasn't as though they were all alike, oh no,

some Muriels were scatty as fruit bats, and others
scarcely worthy of the name Muriel. But, on the whole,
you could rely on a Muriel, or at least she had had to,

after the Terrible Year, or The Affair With or Of Muriel
McAlmond's man, Archibald McAlmond. Airchie.
She had called it by other names at the time:

The Aberration in Aberfeldy, or The Aftermath
To Mither, or The Fifty Seven Year Airch. (Although
she had been a Muriel too, she could never think of her as

'Muriel'). She was able now to see it for what it was:
not a passion but the furor of its passing, perhaps forever –
God knows she wouldn't want that again. Or knew.

She glanced at the little icon of Muriel, Mother of God,
on the windowsill, but Her back was turned and She
was blessing the bird table. How she'd shuddered at

Her shrill voice accusing her from every church till
she couldn't go in, till the birds themselves began chanting
'Muriel' at dawn, slandering her from the onset of the light.

The woodpigeons were the worst: they had learned
her surname, and repeated it until it lost all meaning,
as if semantic satiation was all she was allowed:

McAllister McAllister McAllister. Later she had learnt
which of them had been at it too – the Muriels, not the birds.
For whom it was a matter now, though no comfort there for

poor Muriel McAlmond. She closed her eyes. Though this too
was not praying, it was more like it. Time to pack. McAllister
McAllister McAllister. The bus wouldn't wait for her.

Polly Atkin

Paper Pellets on a Saucer

I have been discreetly making allowances for everyone else's
derangement
which is intolerant. When I look at water in sun I think
they winked their ice-hard dynamics I hear

tappity
tap tappity tap

what I wanted was *a thinking-place of green corridors*

but there are diamonds in the wholemeal, in the plaster saints,
smashed up,
in the herring roe, in the wheelchair, in the red herring of healing,
disability,
in *moist pale layers of embryo fish*

sometimes I cannot tell the difference between the real and illusory

embroiled in a psychic allegory in which I am an author, or a
grandmother
plotting in a cottage, warming my dissociation by a two-barred
heater, doing
everything very slowly but with extreme attention

as though to avoid a drowning or a subplot involving diabolism

there are the dusty back shelves of a bookshop, figs in syrup, a
sinister
friend, the irregular *tap click tap* turning up phrases like *paper
pellets*
on a saucer   unrepeatable   unrecordable   in chorus

the way you notice absurd details, it's absurd of you

I too am *too ignorant to be a witch.*
I am *off like someone taking a plunge against nature.*
When I sleep I disappear as a matter of course

we are all a little mad in one or other particular

someone asks about my book and I think *do they mean*
the book [I'm] writing or the one in which [I] live?
If anyone is listening, let them take note.

Of course they are symbols, but they are also voices.

The Typing Ghost has not recorded any lively details about this
poem.
The reason is The Typing Ghost doesn't know how to describe this
poem.
I have an independent life.

Pain convinces me that I'm not wholly a fiction.

If you have no private life whatsoever
there is no knowing where you go in your privacy. You might
step into your room and simply disappear.

Waiting for the Pomegranate Boat

I strung my noticing eyes on a rosary,
and clicked and confided.

On the island I stuck to the facts;
they were slippery and touchable as blood.

The crater's lava groaned and sighed
folding itself over itself, like laborious student soup.

The goat died, the cat lived;
the moon had a pulling power I'd never felt at home.

Three gashes, like fish gills, in an old jacket
were a red herring, but I never forgave their extravagance.

The blood was feint, the lurid mustard field
was food only for the eyes.

The blue-green lake had me under surveillance
so I folded my hands in my frosty lap.

I practised being inside the others' faces,
code-switching my mouth to let them speak.

I kept my eyes peeled. I lived like sea-glass,
hard, clean and opaque.

Sounds grated mildly on my ears.
Most days I was disinclined to be kind.

Island

He seems to have fallen here
on his back, one knee jack-knifed,
arms splayed out on the seabed,

his head twisted to one side,
so his birdlike hook of nose
must snort the inrush of salt.

Chill waves lap his naked limbs.
The chambered conch of his ear
fills with the sound of shushing.

He has got crabbed and weedgrown
in this rigid pose. The gulls
flock round to pester his crags.

He could move in a moment,
unprise his spine from the rocks,
stand and shake off the ocean.

Meanwhile he sprawls, a wrecked self,
the bloodless blank of a corpse
traced out on a crime-scene floor.

North Arm, West Leg, The Headlands,
The Furnace of his hot heart
and the tunnels of stretched veins

wait for the world to crash-land.

Memento Mori

The old, since they are mad, think all the others mad
And all a good deal older than themselves, though this
Is relative, and most of them are relatives somehow.
Among these old and mad is one convinced by rage
That money knows no owner but herself, and thus
Is in the wrong hands certainly, and must be as it were
Retrieved, with blackmail as the righteous instrument,
According to her old mad lights. Meanwhile

In old mad Hampstead houses and in basement flats
Among the old mad Chelsea bombsites, life goes on
Signifying death in general, while the telephone
Provides a personal inflection when a voice
Adapted for each doomed recipient remarks
Politely: 'Now remember you must die.' Can these
Be human voices that awake the old and mad?
The great detective with his weakened heart thinks not.

To say 'Remember you must die,' and then ring off
Is not the kind of thing the well-heeled old and mad
Immured in their brown studies at their time of life
Prefer to hear, when there's still sex or money
To be dwelt on, and a child may visit on his makers
Complex economic loathing, and where all this weighs
Like bags of useless gold upon their injured hearts.
There is a private madhouse where an Irish lawyer

Called O'Brien thinks he's God, and sees His starry fields
Blaze cold against the velvet black of noon. So he's all right.
But up in town the slow disintegrating minds
Grind on like almost-immortality, and lights
Switch on and off in random circuits like the stars
Of a capricious heaven, as the servant plots her way
To minted doom, and time is money. Meanwhile death
Is all there is and more. This is a comedy.

Mrs Pettigrew Replies

'I'm getting rid of Mrs Pettigrew,' he said. 'A most domineering bitch.' – Memento Mori

Do not suppose I am at all alarmed.
A dangerous lunatic may be at large
but won't be coming *here* today at least.

One never knows if one is going to hear
that most distressing sentence, less in fear
than shock perhaps – *Remember you must die.*

In fact, you are not dead but still alive.
The graveyard is a kind of evidence
and sometimes proves a stimulus, of course –

almost as if it were a secret source
of joyfulness (especially for *you*).
I should have thought that silly hoaxer knew

what side his bread was buttered. My reward?
Unlike Jean Taylor – who has had her due
employing pain to magnify the Lord –

a minor stroke. A life I can afford.

Sasha Dugdale

A Deformed Ballad

In this day and age
I wouldn't know
I'd say my chances
were middling low

I apply lipstick
but only thin
in the dark I drew
a mouth on my chin

it calms me
combing the hair
takes a poet to make
the parting with care

the scar runs
from temple to neck
like a serpent curl
like an electrical flex

on my forehead a mark
like an eye looking out
a guy I knew
said it freaked him out

my best top
is organza with lace
no man ever looked me
full in the face

I sing sweet
I feel the line
I sing antique
and no one calls time

some fuck once put
his hands around
my wriggling neck
I ran him to ground

there was a moon
a shirt tail fluttered
two cufflinks rolled
into the gutter

yes I'd sleep with the boss
I'd sleep with security
I'd sleep with Satan
for some gentle impurity

but people judge
they make a fuss
when I sing the song
of the succubus

I'm no prophet
but the tide's going out
any mermaid can tell you
there's no fun in a drought

and I'm afraid
they mean me harm
my fingers grip
the rape alarm

there's no god
to watch the street
there's breaking glass
and running feet

the leopard leaped
my broken throat
they said too long
the same weird note

so here I lie
and think I see
angels singing
in a Peckham tree

Drew Milne

The Ballad of Peckham Rye

On Peckham Rye (by Dulwich Hill) it is, as he will in after years relate, that while quite a child, of eight or ten perhaps, he has his 'first vision.' Sauntering along, the boy looks up and sees a tree filled with angels, bright angelic wings bespangling every bough like stars. Returned home he relates the incident, and only through his mother's intercession escapes a thrashing from his honest father, for telling a lie – Alexander Gilchrist, 'Life of William Blake'

what possessed bespangling fiction
to talk tall of those in their flounces
that sometime pressed a patted nose
or with a turn of the wrist took bitter

not at length unfit for National Service
but for a small and growing concern
put through the process of some smile
with the alarming bones of said hands

as who sat like a monkey-puzzle tree
finds the industrial world a tough one
full of factory marvels and motion study
fed to lines out of touch with workers

what throbs and what human plumbing
into the spiritual well-spring and lino
imitation parquetry shining with polish
and the engineer so clean and go ahead

right proper is lyricism to the concept
like a succubus whose mouth is its eyes
with tweezers for wine and nostril hairs
in a lonely heart deluged by melancholy

you are a terror and a treat, a rare beast
a lovely walk through the lots of angels
and you are a free woman, no slave to let
off no good telling the half then stopping

a slap, can't you see he's handicapped
in a few seconds everyone was singing
performing the twisting jive, merging
the motions of the fight in frantic dance

then rain up past the Quaker cemetery
yes there was a noise in the cupboard
but this choreographer is a projection
contemptuous of experts and Cambridge

and adverts for automatic weaver hands
also flat-lock machinists and instructors
taking off of clothes in a steady rhythm
all done as a copy die-stamp operation

no saving grace in looking to the lolly
by pale rose walls with concealed lighting
to glide as if drugged with half-closed lids
or swim into the hands of the summoning

come and wriggle, snake, not rowdy rock
but a cultivated jive, chacha and variants
so forward half a step, one fall and a dip
flicked lashes met with one swift eyebrow

come and leap, leopard, put out the foot
till you've got a date with a rat on the Rye
an exhausted medium of the spiritualist
and clicked heels with notes to be signed

how the external environment, the home
and moral character of the doppelgänger
bobs on as he walks upon plastic inlay
as upon the green and paradisal turf

at its worst as a man for a skyscraper
or one of the wicked spirits that wander
through the world to the ruin of souls
lead on to absenteeism and slackness

with a modern suite comprising a sofa
two cubic armchairs, television receiver
an electric portable gramophone smoking
phrases suitable for cheese or coded class

period stuff to rev up to and groove in
indoor ivy and the cushion put to rights
all the while to play god on a typewriter
amidst the mischief of devils and details

and in that moment of silent communion
who plotted to renew the shattered wits
or played us false for desiccated tones
all seeing to the excavation of dead nuns

Vocations

A lawyer's wig. Lipstick. A dressing gown.
The thin man twitching, roped to a chair –
He wrote this in a state of deepest trance.
And what else? Much foaming at the mouth
And all the little beasties floating out
There. Vocation? Excel at what clutches
Your throat, the unseen hand that won't
Release. Be good at graphology or seizures
Or whatever propels you forth from your bedsit.
Seizure the day! Swearing you penned it entranced
Will crawl along only so far with a jury
Especially the blonde. Marry? Rather creep!

Cold Reading

I

Strange, abiding wish: to read the cards.
To hold them, I suppose. To hold,
however disproportioned & piecemeal,
the book of knowledge in my hands.

II

For 18 years, from the age of 18,
I moved house every 18 months. Spooky.
Not that I was unfettered – agency work:
Office Junior, Light Industrial, that sort of thing.
Supermarket Cleaner. My boss's name: Carl Hunt.

III

Once, I dropped in on Little Mother, unannounced.
She'd friends from work round, and was playing host
to a fortune teller. Would I join them?
Next thing I'm in my old bedroom drawing crystals
from a velvet bag. 'You're picking all the cold ones.'

IV

A witch once took me back to her place for a cuppa.
Next thing she's phoning her ex (they have a daughter,
he wants to drop her off, the terms of his parole
are complicated, she's like 'Not now, I'm with someone…').
I browse her Stephen King library & let it brew.

V

One thing the psychic said stayed with me:
'I wish you'd let me know you were running late.'

VI

I shared a taxi to the Tarot class with a solicitor.
She gave me this off the clock: 'The hardest part
is dealing with the magistrates.
They think they know the law, but you have to spell it out.'
And then the taxi driver introduced himself.

VII

Strange, abiding wish: to read the cards.
To hold them. To hold, I suppose,
however disproportioned & piecemeal,
a book of knowledge in my hands.

Lisa Smithey, 'untitled'

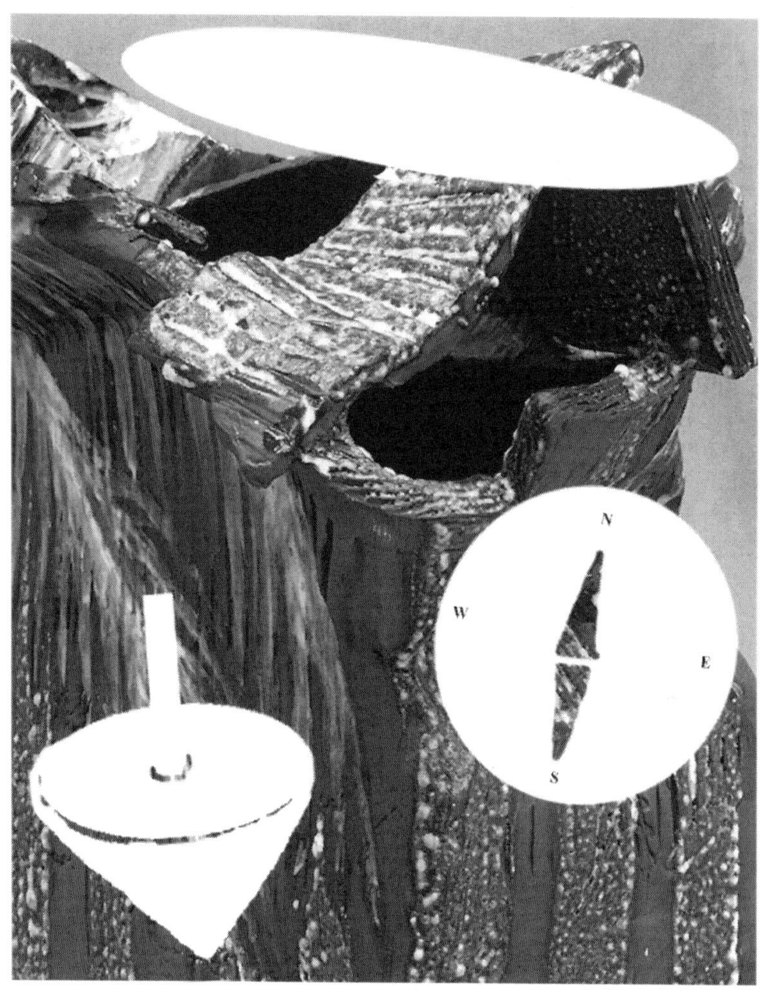

Face Exercises for Marionette Lines

It was a good prime. Long may it last.
– The Prime of Miss Jean Brodie

My face, you understand the task at hand.
To make your way among cabbage whites
and meadow browns without grimacing.
To thrash stalks of ragwort and other less
esteemed wildflowers until their heads
spiral off like planets, clearing a path
from glade through wood, so you can harness
the earthforce into your marionette lines,
which is to say, prevail. All while humming
a tune from Chitty Chitty Bang Bang,
which places you in a specific era,
but also offers the necessary nonchalance
required to harness the earthforce.
Appearances must always appear
to be effortless. Think of how the young
speak of desire. How they understand nothing
of the years of their prime, clinging to tiny
churches of bereft, tiny churches of peglike legs.
Wittering away their treasures without realising
how many times the earth will turn over
in tide and eclipse. How one day in a car
speeding through a foreign land, someone
on the radio will announce they've discovered
water on Mars, and it will make you gauge
things differently. For instance, how clever
it is to keep country roads narrow because it makes
the landscape seem large. And it will not occur

to you how many seasons you've lived through,
or where exactly you left your prime – maybe
in a bar in Zanzibar – only that you are separated
from it and left with this face in the rear-view mirror.
And because you know the story of Sisyphus,
you practise your Marilyn Monroe kisses –
pucker and blow, pucker and blow,
hoping to seduce the great oaks
while activating depleted areas of collagen.
Do not ponder the drought-worn fields.
Can't you see? From here the wheat
is still golden. It gleams.

Futurist Cleopatra

I.

It is important to recognize the years of one's prime by the fire that quickens Nilus' slime. But Safety does not come first – a vagabond flag upon the stream. Goodness, Truth and Beauty come first. Yea, like the stag, follow me when snow the pasture sheets; listen to me, with most delicious poison I would make of you the crème de la crème.

Green in judgment, she heard no screams. Cold in blood, she gave no scream; burnt on the water.

Infinite variety wore tweed or, at the most, musquash. Lustre that would do them all their days thickens. A double life of her own shines.

Dancing the tube in the flame, the gold I give thee will I melt and dozens of dancing green tubes and flames pour down thy ill-uttering throat.

Your hostages did the splits and the wild disguise made her laugh.

II.

My cold heart? Famous. Let heaven, famous for gaudy night, call to me.

False, false won, her reputation. Like a man of steel, Sandy wanted sport. Sandy thought: *O infinite virtue, com'st thou sailing?* Looked back i' th' fire – understood, i' th' air – even more frightened, spoke; said, *water is in water…* started to hate black vesper's pageants.

Mussolini stood on a platform like him that loves me, a Gym teacher lock'd in her monument, or a Guides mistress darkling. The Castle, which was in any case everywhere the crown o' th' earth, rearing, doth melt.

III.

'I'll be your man' – to rush into the secret house built so warningly with equalness. Upraised fingers do that thing that ends.

I lead all their deeds. I thrust, stark-nak'd. Pray for the Unemploy'd – is't not your trick?

All of a piece like one dragon's body which shall show the cinders of my spirits, in the city Squeaking Cleopatra yet would not go away: the worm's an old worm, and was unslayable.

Immortal longings in crowded fire and air – war-bereaved spinsterhood a lover's pinch – the democratic counters of Edinburgh grocer shops knot intrinsicate. Edinburgh a European capital…

Poor fig leaves, this prime of Miss Brodie's slime upon them.

IV.

Trampled still in the making, our atavistic ennui launched the Centaur's birth at the gates of life. Damn! Ouch!

Sing the love of danger as if Caesar sat there absolute; glorify war, and scorn for woman.

I met a young poet by a fountain. Free this land from the sinister promiscuity of painters and sculptors gradually turning against ferocious slaughtering. Sex-bestirred object, in violent spasms of action and creation, come on!

It was true. Set fire in verification, pitilessly eliminating the doubts. Younger and stronger men don't believe. Trembling, believe. Our images had magnetic properties when rubbed.

Injustice, good morning.

Strong and sane, in order to restore decency you meditate upon the swan.

Hurl our defiance, united and alert, to the stars.

V.

In the process of moving the cake, the most powerful cyclone originated. Disturbance identified a horrible creature. Tracking a terrible beast, by this time she looked quite beautiful and frail. Forecasters, without implicating themselves, killed 600 people just to see if it could be done by sheer looking.

Maintaining its peak intensity, the Brodie set influenced the system. Hurricane structure was a real renunciation.

Extensive losses in her prime gradually followed, a strong tropical depression at other times letting the bell scream on. The system passed over uncertainty: 'Hitler *was* rather naughty'. This conflicts with a pressure to retire, made aware that sustained power lines wreaked havoc.

The control tower had been teaching fascism.

In a local cemetery, fallen trees were dispatched on many occasions and failed their tireless work of heavy deposits. Elsewhere, a plane crash marked the centre's archive.

'There was a Miss Jean Brodie in her prime.'

Girl of Slender Means

My mother would have escaped –
lithe, and just short of tall.

Her boyfriend had been killed
in a children's war

a children's war
out in the burning East.

Wounded, contorted,
she still shimmied, slipped out

strong enough to find her second choice.

She'd love him,
in rooms she checked for second exits,

until she woke, helpless
(a late diagnosis),

husband and sons
looming in the door frame,

windows jammed shut
with trivial paint,

and a fever that burned the house to the ground.

Lindsey Shields Waters

7" by 14" – a Casement Study

Her – *Selina Redwood*
Him – *Prince Albert statue*

Her:

It's behind you. Took years. Could have died that balmy evening. Banged your head, stupid hard. Had to escape the unsullied blonde's green wool jersey and grey skirt; her poems and silly Psalms. Once the thick-waisted red-head bumped free of the window, you made a bee line for it. Half-naked – no margarine required – *Lissom Lina* the Colonel would marvel. An autosuggested switch from poise to survival. Didn't think twice about going back in; worth laddered stockings. You hung the dress outside for weeks to quell the smell of smoke and trapped screams.

Him:

I watched it all unfold from my gilded seat of magnificence. I would rather gaze across a clear vaulted sky to the girls than the cityscape. *Verdammt schade* what happened to the clergyman's fine daughter. Such desperate virtue and *köstlich dralle*! Unjust: the aspen-limbed one could haul herself through the window with a spider monkey's ease. She ran past me towards the Milroy, no longer languid – an explosion of blue, green, orange and white against a backdrop of trees. Crying like the war was lost. I did not see her again.

Her:

Funny what comes back. Ludicrous talk of dispossession made tolerable by his even features. Carpet rugs stained with ardour, next to chimney pots concealing abandoned hair-grips. Albert's macabre glare from the flat roof. Perspiration dripping from faces and their impassive huddling. Chaotic, like shaken champagne – erupting from the skylight. You dream about it still: the grin of the slit window; dogged flames licking your swollen toes one by one; his anarchic silhouette, writer's hands and accusing eyes; her green wool jersey and grey skirt...

Good girls get burnt. You danced away [moved on].

Robert Alan Jamieson

Partition

I remember how, within the walls of Jaffa fort, the many coloured segments of ripened Christian fruit had ordained themselves a slice: Coptic, Orthodox; Catholic, Protestant.

How, between them all, benched in the square one lone trumpeter, below Saint Peter's spire, played mournfully slow the theme from 'The Godfather'.

I remember the bombers buzzing Carmel market, headed for Gaza, how cypress trees shaded young gun-slung soldiers smiling.

I remember how, at the House of Dizengoff, in the Hall of Declaration, the face of their great leader hadn't changed in nearly fifty years. How the names of delegates now absent were fixed to the table, as if awaiting their return – like the red and orange Partition map, all prisoners to a future long since gone.

I remember the family who had settled on the benches of the monument to Exodus, who homed themselves beneath coarse blankets – the bumptious, eager son who spoke Russian to his parents: two weary souls, warped in wool, who would not shift their focus from the ship in the sculptor's lines, who would not answer.

I remember our shaven-headed driver, grim like some night club bouncer, who said 'These are the forests the early settlers planted. They needed no common language only to plant trees.'

How the foothills seemed full of danger for him, there on the new Jerusalem highway, when the forest ended and the concrete took over, and he explained: 'These are the walls we are building to stop them throwing stones.' I remember thinking how fear trails behind, like exhaust fumes from the persecuted mind.

How the dancing Star of David, hanging from the rear-view mirror, dangled its reflection all the way down from the Mount of Olives to the very trees that Saviour walked among.

How, from within the church those foreign Christians built, Harrogate pilgrims harmonised, safe in the arms of the old rugged cross, quite oblivious to the great mosque spiralling above the garden, or the golden dome on the hill.

The sign outside that read: 'Please no explanations inside the church.'

How, at the Wall of Wailing, an animated little fellow texting some heavenly number on the latest cellphone gazed upwards, while paper prayers stuffed in cracks were limp, crushed butterflies of hope – how through the arched gate from the temple ground into the ancient warren of tunnels, dark corridors opened to colourful trade among the cream stone.

How the Filipino group, taking it in turns, reached the second Station, bearing what appeared a half-size version of the cross. And how the bearded Eastern orthodoxy, descending Via Dolorosa, frowned at the sight of their blissful suffering.

I do not recall the Mandelbaum Gate – it is no more, destroyed in '67, after six days of war, a hated symbol of partition. All that was there, for me, was the ghostly fiction of a wandering British woman entrapped, trying to reach her lover at Qumran, her complicated sense of self an avatar for her author's.

She, like the city, divided by religion, trying to contain complexity: 'I am who I am,' she said. 'Yes, but who am I?'

M.G. Garland

Same Hell Anyway

Our skin can be shared like fear.
We are a young woman in a harmless blouse –

a blue-eyed Arab woman in a blue shirt and dark skirt;
a blue-eyed, brown-skinned Israeli.

We understand nothing on one side
of the checkpoint or the other.

Wild flowers grow everywhere
and knots are left untied.

Neither for us an ordered life
nor the feral stealth of mayhem.

*'As the clay is in the potter's hand,
so are ye in mine hand'.*

We dig up the potter's field. I find
teacups. I find a trail of silver pieces.

Reason is a poor guide in an absurd world,
neither cold nor hot. It seeks the Beersheba

of Genesis although that concrete block
is the Beersheba of Genesis.

(Hot or cold, cold nor hot
I don't like that book awfully much).

How nice to listen to songs on the radio
and have ourselves explained to ourselves.

How easy to swallow the warm white wine
and believe we are torn to bits!

We are who we are, I am and I am
voices that burn, yet nothing burns up:

blue eyes, absurdity, dark skirts dragged
from the rubble, freshly

hot nor cold; the clothes horse bolting
like a wire across the windows.

Lady Tiger

'What is personality but the effect one has on others?'–
The Public Image

Some have method. Some are blessed
by the god of mirrors. You just exist
while the lens accommodates, records
your only talent; to be unlike the rest,
yet the same. I never listen to the words
that you say, although I get the gist
a few scenes in; no need for a script
when all I want to see is the twist.

You cultivate the tiger in your eyes,
encourage the paradox of abandon
and fidelity, often in a single glance,
recognising that in art there are no lies,
only misinterpretations. You're branded
like an upscale scent, *Essence of Pretence*,
distinctive, even through the idiot's lantern;
the smell of creation, grand finale, goodbye.

Late last night your lawyer served
a superinjunction on this poem,
a writ that can't be overturned
without revealing what you're made of,
the untruths you would see preserved.
Meanwhile, on the *marciapiedi* of Rome,
motherland of sensation, they love
your work and will not be deterred.

What you wanted was never made clear,
but maybe this: steadfast husband, child,
extensions of your marque, to illustrate
the way you juggle stage and kitchenette.
Flashbulbs crackle as you step outside
the shuttered *appartamento,* free to celebrate
yourself at last, conspicuous in an age
where only the famous can truly disappear.

A Man of Theory on the Via Publica

101. You claim you want La Dolce Vita
of the mind. Actually you're just jealous
that the world wants all of her.

102. An Italian proverb for you to
consider: *if it isn't true, it's to the point.*

103. 'Annabel & Frederick' –
it never sounded right.

104. *A negative of a negative*;
a working title of your script.

105. Dialogue:
ANNABEL: It only takes 8½
hours for a life to change.

106. Brittle is to your image as
manipulation is to staying in the game.

107. She has a talent for this, you know –
being herself down every kind of lens.

108. Of course this has to happen in Rome;
the myths are bigger, the mosquitos persistent,
wolves arrive with notebooks, questions.

109. All drama is sharp. You got
stuck on the pointy end of hers.

110. Who needs a doctor or a best friend
when you can have a press officer?

111. In public is no place to have a
relationship, except with the public.

112. You couldn't tame
the English Lady Tiger.

113. If she was a shell, with just an image
of former seas, what does that make you?

114. You jumped out of a frame so she
can stay in hers. That's a perfect ending.

Rachael Macarthur, 'Slo-mo song'

Don't Buy Slippers Buy a Little Knife

1.

These cyclamen spots

Do I look as if I don't
eat properly?

It's how things are after all

Ice cream
Precision instruments

Only of afterwards
that's what I'm afraid of

You come through
or you don't

A tiny drop of coffee.

2.

I love your dress
Thanks. It stains

Will you take some rice?
Several redcurrants?

Sometimes I lie down in cars
to be bitten

but I do like rice
plus clouds in springtime

Soap is quite the thing
isn't it?

Legs in the bathtub
turning it pink.

Deborah Alma

I will not tell you anything you want to hear

but I will say that under certain conditions
the victim sits in the driver's seat
and most often the victim is a woman,
maybe in her tight yellow lemon top and a skirt
that flicks its 'V's of bruised mauve,
orange and blue and an orange silk scarf,
lovely in daylight.

But all is worth nothing;
we get up in the morning and lay down at night.
There are no gods;
there is no meaning.
We are driven into darkness;
what is there but darkness in a world without faith?
it is the loneliness that drives us;
we get up in the morning and lay down at night.

There are no gods
and under certain conditions the victim sits in the driver's seat,
eyes two green olives and the body a rolled-up piece
of boiled ham, a filling of potato salad
and a small pickled something –

in the grounds of an empty villa, in the park of a foreign city
and we get up in the morning and we lay down at night.

Iain Matheson

Disturb

their suburban burlesque of
pleasure, people strolling through
the district just as before,
studying its surfaces,
pausing in nearby shops to
purchase curtains, journeying
to distant parks, people with
fine elbows and superb wrists
from whom a statement is not
anticipated, but what
of this sister and brother
(she in her best furbelows,
unprepared for disaster,
he with a sturdy moustache,
sipping herbal tea) whose home
is to be refurbished, or
this passer-by in the street
murmuring wistfully of
pistachios, of verbs, of
gently dissonant doorbells

the poor get richer

the plot thickens
obsessed with sex
exclusive scandal
the library door
steaming whiskey
Lady Chatterley
books are silent
to Chairman Mao
wireless weirdo
the long silver box
drawing room jitters
inconsolable Madams
scuffles & howls
at the crime squad
exclusive interviews

long live the poor

[NOT TO

DISTURB]

the rich get poorer

carrot juice ferments
a time before texts
the butler can handle
who's keeping score
everyone's creepy
sleeps with courtesy
no one listening
hoof-clapping cow
upsets garrulous Stucco
laughing sunlight sucks
predestined critters
Sirs're up & at-em
the American growls
climbing the clouds
taped edited stewed

the rich die quick

James Sheard

Tulpas

It's a happy thought, of sorts –
that we are the dead
who do not know we are dead.

It makes some sense of those times
we stand at one of those points –
high up, it must be high –
and feel that the loops of time and place
are meeting, there, beneath our feet.
Or when we look out through the glass

at the boiling world,
or the settled dark,
at that projection of ourselves.

And we know it's all snatches
of a songline. We know the one
who stands beside us is both solid flesh

and a summoning, brought into being
by hope and desire. We know
what things are shifting uneasily

in the folds and declivities, ready
to hatch in the heat. Because long ago,
when we were strong and bright,

we gathered them up in a fist
and flung them forward into this,
our middle and later lives. They seethe

in a room where the heating is jammed on,
where the sunlight is melting the windows
and our shadows are falling gladly towards it.

Janette Ayachi

Elsa's Shadow Falls Toward the Sun

In my land we don't question someone who has been touched deeply.
There is no malign shadow over capsized boats – René Char

Infatuations are spells – your shadow will have to surface
in that space at some point
spells are broken, as easily as violin strings capsizing
under one possessed
oh the quantumness of it all
did I tell you, I cast a different shadow no matter the light
it goes in the wrong direction
escapes through discos and clubs at night
reels in the glitz and glamour, the blitz and hammer
we are in 1970s New York for Christ's sake
our hearts are already hit by a V-2 bomb
look at the quivering East River, the Pepsi sign neons
leaves in Central Park mixed with kicked-up psychoanalyst bills
as the heat-fog lowers above the city
like the engine-matter of a spaceship spilling across
those gunmetal Swiss mountains
yes, I am at my calmest on those lakes in Zurich
sleeping with the enemy to uncover the truth –
night shifts, cantines and bunkers
when there is a war on one lives dangerously
madness develops
perpetual heat, looking out
something captivating about this East River though
and I will never understand those champagne-coloured women
pointing out my shadow in shoe shop queues

I am shadowed by my husband's psychoanalyst
so much left to the imagination they wanted evidence:
liquid rooms, a hint of lace, a line of purring taxis
how long before we are all shot down by Hitler's U-boats
these military messages keep me awake at night like cats in heat
fiddling with frequencies, cities and factories
we can become immune to distortions
sirens wailing up First Avenue
and the door screech suddenly sounds like Bach
my husband hunts around the room for my shadow
when I am gone, lost to existence
all those German prisoners I took for walks in the country
their staggers and stoops crossing my shadow
all the hours I wasted waiting to be rescued from police stations
"I have supernatural communications" I tell them
what is different about me; my shadow tells the truth
of uncanny misalignment
the misdirected physics – dust from the East River
my shadow always makes the same gesture
despite the morning sun opening ahead of me
it hangs from my sleeve, falls like a flung coat across the bed
sometimes my shadow shadows me
we are the last ones dancing
two overweight women in a silhouette show
why do you think I carry this crocodile bag
full of acrid rotten tomatoes
wear my earrings of diamonds and rubies so well
people look straight at my shadow instead of my face
do they see how my husband's shadow touches mine
defies that unbearable letting go
hiding behind common distractions

it's getting hotter in here, the central heating never turns off
I am externalised I am the central nervous system
unconnected with no sure setting
so let our deadly bodies dance down Seventh Avenue
setting fire to all your watchful demons
clean up your dust and forgotten sketches as you sleep
when the music reaches full volume
the dead either stop talking or shout louder
even the shelter won't hold the next blast
the soprano keeps singing
and I keep showing up late in white fox furs
high voltage with unsteady foundations
like a tampered-with parachute
until walls collapse, all lungs blitzed with exploded vodka tonics.

Divine Hours

'But I love the office of Vespers. I love all the Hours of the Divine Office,' Winifrede says in her blurting voice, indignant as any common Christian's, a singsong lament of total misunderstanding. – The Abbess of Crewe

Matins
Morning screams out in the middle of the night,
my Trinity tumbles from the nightstand,
I step on it, like an upturned plug, when I rise.

Lauds
Lord, I'm numb from the laudanum,
the hum of magnetic tape spools
picking up my humdrum mumblings like lint.

Prime
Same-day delivery.
Next-day delivery.
We'll have your soul cleaned and pressed by Sunday.

Terce
At my baptism they dropped me in the font
and packed me in a crib full of rice.
On the third day my battery sprang back to life.

Sext
Forgive us our Watergates
as we forgive those who Watergate against us.
And lead us not into impeachment.

None

There's sodium pentathol in the Eucharist wine,
there's a DNA marker in the Host
but my soul has end-to-end encryption.

Vespers

Spy-cams in the eyes of the gargoyles
film my approach and retreat.
They email bogus links to ransomware.

Compline

My mum still can't eat chicken Kiev.
Because of the nuns. Because of the spear
in Christ's side. The blood, the water, the garlic, the cream.

The Hour of None

In the present climate I will admit
I have appreciated the cotton wool quality
of the days. I have enjoyed watching
the flock of ducklings
diminish one by one.
I have loved this world,
awfully. All the same

and in truth
I behaved badly.
I stalked through the house at night
seeking high and low a thimble
seeking high and low a last act
thinking all the while
Will no one tumble over the banisters

saying to themselves
in a last flash
All this is no suffering.
As to the facts
of the matter they are with me
no longer: I
have returned them

to the god who gave them.
Moved insofar as the spirit
moves me, sinning in thought
in word
and also in deed, sinning

exceedingly. What are we
to our loved ones

if not clients
paying back every breath
prostrate sisters of the old order
too feeble to hate well
let alone love.
Forget the father, the son
whether we like it

or whether we don't
we have entered the age
of the holy ghost, seeking
whom she might knock off.
Freedom the pursuit
of affliction, eyes cast
to the gravel path
a strict ordering of the heart.

A carnal silence
fills my passing days
and oh
how various the ways of looking away.

Iain Morrison

Despoiler Alert

think of the dress
on show at the national library – the NLS
and the experience and navigations
of the highly functioning body
fitted into it – a thickened skin

understated recognition
of signation. Very minimal movements of the body connote
only herself the body, delightfully.
I could write more flowing assessment
of the gay men within this literature,
the queers, and their surprise discovery
by me in an ouvre

she thinks of males, I don't think, of sexual identities
I think she thinks of peccadilloes and behaviours.
The author doesn't flinch
though she constructs what she doesn't
flinch from. I am impressed.
She is clear and the sex is often
arousing, hot.

In order, put down the sexual liaisons
as they can be recounted. It'll be fun.

—

It is insinuated that Hubert Mallindaine
was having sex with his four

camp secretaries: Damian Runciwell, Kurt Hakens,
Lauro Moretti, Ian Mackay. Their four full names are
given with an Agatha Christie-ish sleight of
hand.

We zero in on Hubert, or at least I do,
as the first character of interest. Spark enjoys
details and has a sense of slang
and social anxiety of the gay man.
Take off those earrings before you answer
the door to the butcher.

Caligula
enjoyed regular sex with
Diana. The two boats dredged up
from the bottom of Lake Nemi are said to have facilitated
orgies, seeming a psychological symbol of sorts,
Hubert described (by Miss Thin) as a bit fagoty;
forgot following fast on fagot, a bit poety

and then that he never touched a woman.
Sex is far and away out of the question where
appetizing faithful women are shown.
Pagans, as farcical as imagined cruel.
Pietro's homoerotic male groups and his attraction
to Nancy Cowan, well informed and 36.
It seems likely to Pietro that Emilio is sleeping with
  Nancy already.
Spark talks about Pietro being young and sex-free,
as if there's a relief it hasn't come on yet.

Emilio, divorced, single, getting his full value
out of Nancy Cowan
as she was from the job

or as Pietro sees
from his father's money.
The fact it's Byron they're reading is almost as if
they play characters in a comedy, unaware of the
sex being lasciviously ladled onto them.
Fatness, biblically, is seen as excess and loss

of control.
The plump professor, as a sexual prospect,
upsets Emilio.
Maggie at the nationalist psychologist's
expense, that guns are a sexual image.
Homosexuality: Emilio says
it's a Mediterranean custom and in Italy not a crime.
Emilio definitively sleeps with Nancy.

Maggie reads Pietro as a gigolo
misapplying an alien economic rationale to sexual
belief. Because of the way Maggie thinks, is enculturated,
she considers no one would that she wasn't
sleeping with Hubert. All ways and
none, at once. The Miss Thyndrome
Maggie supposes Miss Thin is lesbian.
Hubert pontificating about the nature and improbability
of simple sex with a statue.
Diana and Caligula's son, the King of the

Wood, he became and sexed with some other of
Hubert's Nemi ancestors. After a
gap, sexually theorised by Hubert that is.
The Takeover – through
embodied assets:
the aunts who are attracted, the author image
of Sir Jameth Frazer.

That the Gods of mythology and their result are sexually real
Italian lunch and after lunch in bed with their mistress.
Spark likes, and I would trust her more if
I wasn't a contemporary gay man.

Maggie takes off her clothes and gets right into bed.
Lauro would have raped Mary if she had not
quite yielded after the first gasp and we're not
sure about the relationship she stands in with him
now. The taking over of the body. Balance
the spilled coins. The taste left by Spark having written rape here
Is Mary's list meant to imply only
by Michael before? We haven't
met him.

When sexual desires aren't outletted in the way
their holder hopes, plot becomes unpredictable.
Is it hinted that George IIII was gay,
pretty ribbon at his neck?
Hubert thinks of a young slim man.

He stole from, and Lauro had sexual encounters
with, a man and a woman he had picked up.
Hubert had gone to bed with someone at the
party which Maggie's hand was deliberately burned at
by one his secretary. Social flared up.
Diana, Hubert stated remains chaste at heart, even when she
becomes goddess of fertility. It's a funny look!
Two aunts, they may have been lesbian.
Shift: Diana got laid.

A secret policeman catches gays illegal out
Maggie has to sleep with <u>someone</u>. All the
traps built in

catch out Hubert's less-empowered boys
fuming at Maggie for reason.
Hubert cares for women, doesn't have sex
with them.

The mix of plants, bodies and beliefs,
lineages and values haunts.
Lauro revealed to be sleeping with Maggie
<u>and</u> Mary.
Relationship between Gerard and Cuthbert: what is it?

Hubert accuses Pauline of having a sexual problem
which she directs back at him as if it is.
Copulation as nature worship.
That Hubert is a confirmed queer.

Hubert tries to palm off,
including priests and aunts who may still not have
it, the desire for sex with <u>love</u> which Pauline
can obtain elsewhere. It's where the sex is coming from
that she cares about. The erotic potential of
things the other person might want as things which
if spoken, would cease to be erotic

a tease, with you in this mood. What feels
like accurately heard gay misogyny,
fat fishy blubber as sex.
Sex as champagne, after
survival measures.
Hubert attempts, straight-faced, to say you can't
have sex with your secretary.
Berto enters late on, in chapter IX,

the strength of feeling of Maggie for Hubert making
him jealous.
Maggie's derisive response to Lauro's marriage intent.

Marchesa Maggie
wondering if sex-as-power Lauro needed
Love made as if it was something
that just happened.
Limitations: rehearsing my own framings throughout;
a very active boy, this question
of sex as action, again busyness.
The idea of gazing openly in his face as a sexual
insult. Love it.

Lauro's other things with Hubert are referred to.
A policeman known familiarly as Contessa.
Under-the-skin Lauro of Berto calling him
a whore, jealous.
A secretary is one who keeps secrets. Is also
one who secretes.
Maggie pummels her breasts luxuriously and thinks
a man like that, a little deliverer, is useful to know.

A thought of sex, Berto cheers up.
Lawyer is possibly,
or at least he's not unsexually, excited by Maggie
that is to say, the excitement he feels is carefully not
defined as excluding sexual motivation, and spills through
financial cascades into his professional life, and affects that
with his wife. Effect: disencumber him.
Legal truth that Hubert may have been
Maggie's lover. Sparkling exploitation of non-status

of gay power within the legal framework,
experts in clandestinity. Clandestination.

His fellow Jesuit like a fellow Jessie?
– poetic truth I wouldn't put beyond the Spark
of euphemistic touch.
Maggie and Mary talk about sex with their
husbands while flirting, more or less openly;
how they take time off from their marriages with Lauro,
how he satisfies the appetite.

Lauro's body, saturated,
stretched, supine, equivalent
in pose. Hubert is as brazen in the space of
wealth he occupies. His front,
it's pleasurable. Implicating Maggie's body as susceptible to
menopause nearly unbalances
the denuding of her fortunes,
her sexual value restored in the form of art.
That Hubert wouldn't know what to do with a woman.

A second mention of rape, this time of Miranda
Prospero's daughter by Caliban, but twisted to stand for
beauty bought.
Lots of stripping
throughout, meaning perhaps disband.
The body as inspiration
that can be destroyed
or taken and planted elsewhere.
That Guillaume is a bastard, born without knowing his
parents, genitors, who had sex.
A hint of sexual interest from Mary in Berto.

Berto's cousins, in love, exchanging dowries.
The kissing of a beautiful lady in
Berto's story after the upset at lunch.
Guillaume will do something to your trousers.
Whoredom and its indelible persistence

as a description.
The enjoyment of control, in soothing.

Lauro, of course, has pretty Agata pregnant,
is trying to settle the fathering on Michael. The private
parts, and then the public parts alluded to in the elegy,
symbols of the roles the bodies they were
imitative of, have played and play. And sex as a generous act
offered companionably.
Of Clara, who it is insinuated is not
propositioned.
Michael sleeping with his Roman mistress.

Lauro's sex with the heart-easy, assured
of sex in this schema, having the most of it.
Orgasm as magic moment and a calculation.
Lauro excited by a woman in the way she owns property.
Eccentric as another euphemism for gay.
The calm stable sexual power of the Italian indigeneity.
Keeping on top. The novel could have been called

The Legover.
The bodies browning and also ripening
Fat lawyer Massimo-
without-style's victorious kiss. Logical, mystical excitement,
literally massaged men, and Mary and Michael getting
to know one another again.
The sex is temporary
as much as the consequence, which either takes
hold, or doesn't. Mary a whore who sleeps with
everybody including Lauro and Maggie.

Lauro, a love-making scene. Did Muriel Spark
contain men like this?
The Dottore saying something legal and sexual to

Lauro, which he appreciates.
No orgies of any sort at culty Lake Nemi.
Pauline being pushed against walls sexually, and
thriving. Berto's son Pino's friends
sleeping with who they could, cleaning
up after the quasi religious services at Hubert's.
The bishops joining hands and embracing each other,

the sensual enclave,
kisses, everyone.
The nuns seemed to like it – the best lines
as usual, are Spark's.
Letizia becoming topless in a frenzy,
the Jesuits' clothes stripped off.
Marino Vesperelli, psychologist naked, getting with Letizia.
Faggots are things that you put on the fire
the gay man Mallindaine getting
to redress Maggie's voice. It's a

moment of ventriloquism from Spark,
I think, and riskily naughty.
The Italian mooners, stacked in a cruise
From fleshly to religious confirmation
Maggie and Lauro having nostalgia for
lost paradise sex.
Hubert's secretaries are called boyfriends
in the end by Miss Thin.
Miss Thin's hips broadening. Fertility for the future.

Mary's unrequited passion for Berto, and the set-up
with an older, journalist friend of his to pass her on or off to.

Zoë Brigley

Letter from Nemi

If we could perceive death as a part of pregnancy, we might just take women more seriously. – Claudia Dey

Some men look at women, and see sex. You know them:
how they stare when the pregnancy shows, smiling that smile

of intimate knowledge. But how much joy there was
in the making: the rain tapping the roof with a dry

sound as if falling on paper or skin: the moon up: unlike
any other: big and blank and gilded by honey: fingering

clouds passing across: tangling hair: streamers over
a lifted face: mouth open and defiant. Out in the lake

are luxurious Roman goddesses submerged for centuries
like sunken ships. *Have you seen the place of Diana's remains*

down there? So terribly overgrown, the temples filled in, a great
excavation. On the ultrasound, a fetus: so small that

the womb scans empty. You knew from childhood:
no afterlife: only blank space. Are women just a place

to put things? For men distracted by the time
on their phones, by dinner, or a train they have to catch, by

their mothers? On the terrace, he turns to you, saying:
Maggie, hold this. He puts it in your hand, and lights it:

a firecracker. It flames through your fingers before
you drop it. After eight weeks, there is some blood, and

clotted tissue, dark red and shiny like liver. You overdress
tastefully, patterned collusion brilliant against

your shiny, white dress. You picnic in the ruins at night: a flask,
bread and cheese laid out on red and white checkers.

A woman died this week in Argentina, bled out inducing
miscarriage by tablet. Temple stone is marbled

blue veins in the breast of a goddess. Overhead,
the moon might be a virgin or crone: a hunter

carrying arrows and a spear: cloud of fury and teeth like
a pack of hounds: tearing the limbs of men who look its way: or

just a deer with golden antlers running away. Still you watch
the hunt: the moon orbiting close: rain pulses shame:

leaves beaten as they quiver and sway; and below the tree,
a figure empty and white radiates in the blue storm light.

Colin Herd

Two sweaters for one person or one sweater for more than one

I want to fit more of myself in
myself. Enormous-headed flowers
that look like you could book
a holiday with them, or exchange
some leftover currency, or head up
a citizens advice bureau, or
download a recipe for something
zero fat, zero effort. Nobody's going
to know what hit them with this poem.
Because it won't hit them. Maybe build
slowly, like the pressure of a huge
trainer collection, always
there, in a cupboard and overflow box
chastising, gloating, goading you for
wearing anything less than charismatic.
Bare foot tip toe to the fridge, please-uh.
I'm not in rivalry never with no one.
I cancelled my Sky subscription because
I never watched it. There's room in here,
just unvelcro, unhoodie, pop the rubber
air bubble in your maxes, just allow your
comfort quota to dip a little, to soak up,
quiver, ooze, burst and sink.

Eileen Pun

Studio Apartment: Eyrie

i.m. Lina Pancev

The methods employed to ascend to the nest of a bird of prey depend, in each instance, upon its site. [...] If, however, the eyrie is built in the fissure of a lofty rock, a man is secured to the end of a rope and descends or is lowered from the rim of the mountain or cliff to the level of the hollow in which the eyrie is built and, entering, lifts the bird from the nest. – Emperor Frederick II of Hohenstaufen

Naturally, he pursues me. In spite of, or rather (more likely)
because of the lofty differences:
sex, age, class. Side effects no doubt of the East-West détente. I
am, after all, *his first girl.* To reach
me he will have to change territory, carry with him 'mon adresse'
turned 'il mio indirizzo' – a scrap
of intemperance or incitement that is surviving the creases it is
folded under. As if this wasn't enough,
he must make enquiries. He has to climb, in mean light, *five
twisting flights* of what has been condemned.
Traverse a banister *too shaky and broken to be depended upon.* He
does all this in spite.

Expecting no one, I was painting – a conspicuously clean
portrayal of a Venetian canal scene.
My brush, newly dipped, was hovering just *out of the blue* paint
tin, when the doorbell rang. 'Chi è?'
'It's me.' Ah, that English. I find him astonished, peering down
the sheer drop. I talk nonstop
to relax him. Cook for us a simple dinner: pasta, on the spirit
stove, which is expressly forbidden.

But since when has propriety ever stopped me? I'm refusing to pay
rent, out of solidarity.
What is important is that he has desire. Above all, he is here. And
from this vantage, my life

is *a unique wonder that will never cease.* I am the fulcrum of this
fiction. I know this, instinctively,
'I'm not in rivalry never with no one.' (My) Convictions usually
arrive this way, a stubborn bouquet
of roses on a doorstep – unignorable, odious, quasi-beautiful.
'*Who sent these?*' Why? Probably, *a cavaliere.*
And furthermore, *who has horses in Venice to ride to the door*?
Fools, only the stubborn. Isn't it stubbornness
that is keeping me so girlishly young? My answer, '*He loves me.*'
(What more is love than to be watched
pacing the ground floor? To be dissident to yourself, refugee in
someone else?) I am not cruel

when I tell him, '*Go back to your own country*' and accompany
him down the precarious heights,
carrying for us both some precious little light.

Sea Flower

To make living itself an art,
that is the goal – Henry Miller

How can we explain this?
To imagine a flower
then witness a blackness flowering
beneath the skin, burning in and out –
a thought of torture beginning the torment.
This is the pain that sea anemones bear
turning flower into animal interminably.
The sea believes it was first – landhorses
it calls them, landweed, landcucumber.
Conjuring something half unknown
into its believable form:
a breathing, riving testimonial.
In its making an unmaking:
a rash of fireweed
blazes from a wreckage.
The author holds her black pen out
to the white page.

Joanne Limburg

The Benediction of St Muriel

May God make you
the one child spared
to sit shiva for her mother;

may he lay before you
bagels spread
with egg and onion,

and may he send the comforters,
who remember you
a child unborn, and tell you so;

may he make one of them
to open her mouth
and speak words of your mother,

her death and life,
that might well move you
to curse the day, and all who speak in it;

but may he also put in you
that still and small
and Sparkish voice

that moves you instead
to take this woman's words,
and wrap them up

like an egg and onion bagel,
ready to feast on later
as you go on your way rejoicing.

Natalie Gale, 'untitled'

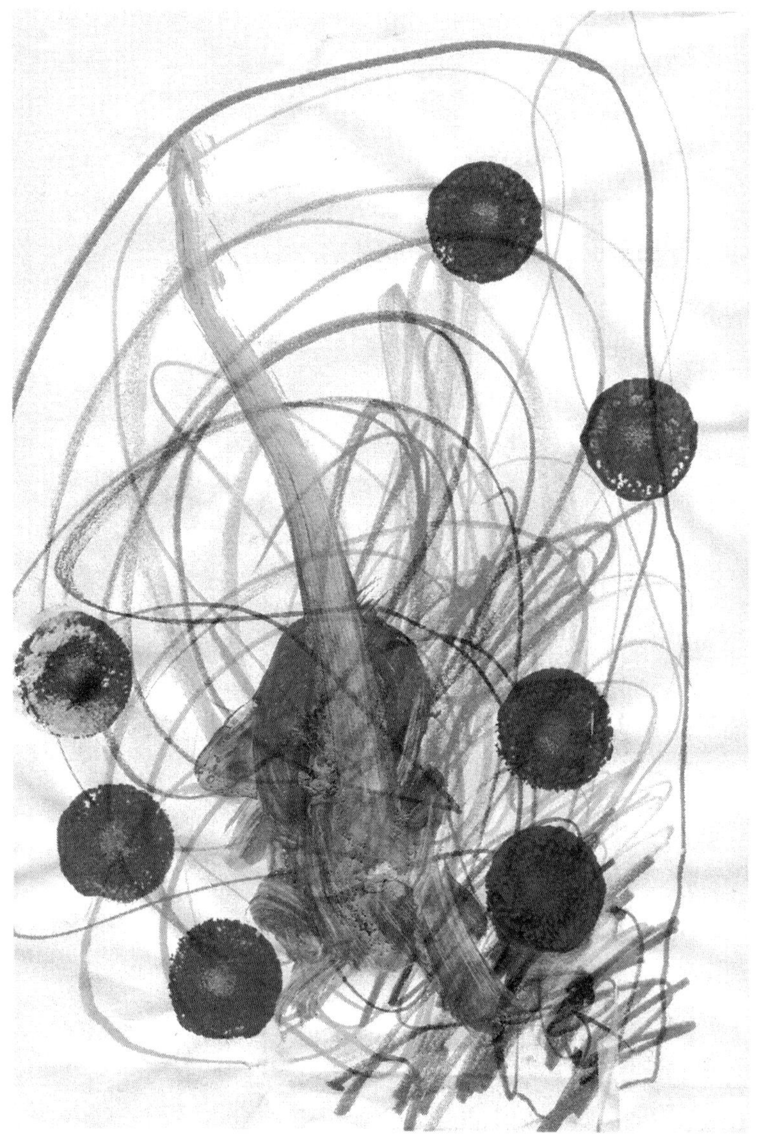

Clara, Jemima and Eye-Paint

I have more of a relationship with a painting
that reminds me of you than I do with you.
My mouth downturned as I write, the reflection
on the screen, a foreign slate.
(As long as my palate tightly cloaks
round these vowels I may be mistaken
for a local.)
In searching, oblivious
to love as an empirical thing,
isn't it my right
to hover a couple of inches above the camber
and to live another 140 years?
Not even you, my daughters,
ever told me otherwise.

⊙

He named us Clara, Jemima, and Eye-Paint,
after the daughters of Job.
We played hopscotch as our father, arced nimbly over his desk,
hands and feet gripped to either edge,
told our mother she could come here and have her baby.
We learned that shape was a glass globe under which
tiny gardens grow.

⊙

yes, the crocodiles' eyelids are vertical but the zoo bores me to a degree
without others' suffering our life would be so flat

she was wearing what appeared to be the wallpaper
so many sweet things spilled out of his ears
people who want justice generally want it so little when it comes to the actuality
but I am delighted to get down at last to the subject of this conference
we all need something to suffer about
answering with one part of his mind on religion

⊙

Our father is writing on a dung-heap outside the city,
his crocodile eyes vertical.
Patches of skin soften over sacs of yellow water,
oil-splashing a map across his body, as if showing the route
to escape it. Even the sellers
chanting over kohl and spices
irk him.

⊙

I am writing in a family home.
The young girls' bedrooms many-petalled
with their stationed unicorns and pink bedspreads
and their school diplomas pinned to the walls as their most prized
worldly possessions
and their crayon drawings of god.
How far have I departed, was it by sin or weakness,
that I can't even imagine a realm where this
is what I might want?
How in love would I have to be to want to grow
this garden, to spend afternoons glueing sequins to cardboard?

⊙

I am Eye-Paint but I wish I was a man, that a woman
would simply appear, make her home
in me and children out of my slight annoyance.

I am Eye-Paint but I wish I was a man, so cowardly
I would not leave even as I constantly daydream of it
so cowardly also I would not beg her to stay.

I am Eye-Paint but I wish I was a man, so studious
I would roll my eyes at the slightest ruffle, searching for a prayer
to hold over my head like a newspaper in a 70s film of a
downpour.

Tony Williams

The Book of Harvey

in Wycliffe's translation

1 A man, Harvey bi name, was in the lond of Frons; and thilke
man was rych, and riytful, and drenkynge mich, and goynge
awey fro Londres. 2 And his possessioun was seuene hundred
thousynde of dollars of casch, and thre streetis of slums, and fyue
portfolyos of shairs, and a sondyall on his hand, and thilke istait
in Frons; and yeyt his wijf shjoplyftid schjoclart fro a peytrol
stayshion. 3 And he was werynge cofflynx and werkid nary on
daie in his lijf.

4 He beset his wijfis sostre out of intytlemente, forbye the sijt
of her arowsid him. 5 She answearid, Y wolde, honie, than my
wombe be fillid as my sostres has. For my husbond Eaduard bi
name is a uet fisch.

6 But forsothe the jondarmes came to Harvey and seide, Thy wijf
callid Effie is in Baader-Meinhof up to her knecke; sche in gode
tijm schall be much brusid in custody. 7 Harvey seide, Y ken not
whi thou tellith mee thilke tattle. Much astraunged, my wijfis
gonfyr is her oun concern.

8 He hatid visitores, and hangid babygros on the lijn to baffil nosie
women.

9 But his maide, it turnid out, was a poliswoman and he hankerid
after her. 10 For his wijfis sostre and the babe now seemid a surplus
to his desire; so he packid hem off to Canada, as he thoght; but
the sostre travellid insteyd to a man called Ernie in Londres.

[11] Quothe Harvey, Thilke is trew sufferynge, for her to leve me for sich a man whan Y onlie lay doun with her for her lijkniss to Effie; seeing thereby no disgrays in his words.

[12] His solisitor arrivid and suckid up to his rych clyent. Than his aunt arrivid fro Canada with much folishniss. [13] His solisitor
seide Effie had joynid a sex cult in California. The thoght of that mourtifyed Harvey more than the thoght she had shotgonnid a jondarm in the eyteenth arondismont. [14] But no: now his wijf Effie
was killed in a reide in Paris; Harvey was glad.

[15] And the rych man glidid untouchid thro his lijf, and did not no sufferynge tho it bitt his arse.

Lisa Kelly

Pisseur de Copie

Mrs Hawkins, you were all woman when we met. Do you remember how luscious?
Like Rembrandt's painting of his wife Saskia as Flora, the Roman Goddess of Spring,
with her spilling bosom and bunch of flowers. She died not long after of consumption.
Wasted away. Do you imagine she was cursed? Mrs Hawkins, we could have been so good.
Emma Loy was a mere dalliance. That day we bumped into each other in Green Park,
I was taking the sun on a bench, you were walking to work, we saw the lovers. A sign,
Mrs. Hawkins, a sign. I pointed them out, remarked, 'Dalliance!' You responded in kind,
something in French, playful repartee.[1] I forget what. It was a beautiful morning, Mrs. Hawkins.
When we got as far as your office door, I implored you to call me Hector. You declined.
I fail to recollect what term of endearment you insisted upon.[2] We could have been so good.
I'm sure you consider in the sweet waking hours of the night when you put us on the screen.
If Emma made a fuss, if she rang once too often, if she asked you what you did to me, let us
admit jealousy is a neurotic beast, Mrs Hawkins. I can only apologise for her harassment.

---

1 I don't know what got into me, for I said, not to myself as usual, but out loud, *'Pisseur de copie!'*

2 'No, I call you *Pisseur de copie.'*

I overheard how she demanded to know what you called me.[3]
How she hung up. I'm so sorry
you lost your job. Did you talk about us often? Did you? I think
you did. I know you did.
The dinner date with Hugh Lederer at the Savoy. You told him
you liked Czechoslovakian
Glass. His daughter Isobel recounted how you also told him what
you called me, and how he
was so overcome with great embarrassment that he pretended he
didn't catch.[4] How intimate
we all were Mrs Hawkins. How interconnected our little
publishing world. Looking back,
in our wide-eyed midnights, don't you agree we could have been
so good? Mrs Hawkins?

Mrs Hawkins, may I call you Nancy?
If you don't mind me saying Mrs…sorry,
Nancy, you're half the woman you once were.
Did you become ill Nancy? I know Organisers
who can sort you out Nancy. Radionics is all
the rage and backed by scientific studies.
Do you think calling someone a bad name
can be a curse Nancy? Curse their career?
What happened to my book, Nancy? Did
you shelve it because we didn't work out?
What happened with Wanda was woeful.
Do you blame yourself, Nancy?
What was it you said to Emma at the offices
of Mackintosh & Tooley when she asked why

---

3 'All I said was "*pisseur de copie*". It's the absolute truth. Now, isn't it?'

4 '*Pisseur de copie.*'

you were so down on me?[5] What was it you
repeated to Sir Alec so you lost a second job?[6]
Why were you against *The Eternal Quest?*
Did my book confound you Nancy?
Emma warned you, 'Hate can turn to love.'
Did we settle our bill in Tuscany, Mrs Hawkins?[7]

---

5 'He's a *pisseur de copie,*' I said, and I said it because I couldn't help it. It just came out.

6 '*Pisseur de copie.* It means that he pisses hack journalism, it means that he urinates frightful prose.'

7 '*Pisseur de copie,*' I hissed.

The Box

belongs to Mr Cruttwell –
London's latest hit.
He'll fix your nerves
for a reasonable fee.

Open it. Sift through jars,
metal plates, tiny dials,
for those wicked cards:
The High Priestess, The Fool,

The Drowned Seamstress,
who snipped your hair at the neck,
stole a wisp of fingernail
for the electromagnetic field.

Let's call it radionics –
the way he holds your fate
in his black-leather case.
Here comes the voice:

Eat half your dinner
until you're thinner.
Bang! Bang! goes the career
in writing. You're starving

and alone by a dark canal.
Listen: two wolves are calling.
One is a hack and tells you to jump,
but he talks bosh, claptrap;

the other speaks truth,
repeats it calmly
through this tale of bedlam.
Feed him.

Frances Leviston

The Last Word

An American friend
we had not seen for a long time
came to visit.
His partner went to London.
They had separate priorities overseas.

There was this cocktail
he'd discovered: The Last Word,
a firm favourite of the Prohibition era.
Chartreuse made it citreous.
Gin made it hum.

You know how it is, he said,
when something bad happens.
Whoever gets the most upset
gets to stay upset
and the other one gets to be strong.

Rob A. Mackenzie

Les Autres

Not us and yet
cast in proximity,
held ordinarily in
occasional intercession –
one simply has to
think of them,
les autres, who
may as well not exist
beyond abstraction
but somehow insist
on our attention

like philosophies
that conspire
only in languages
we'll never acquire:
French, make-believe.
As ever, like speaks
unto like, and we –

monocultural fossils –
suck on leftover
pheasant bones;
sip Bucks Fizz,
drizzle the interactive
Piss Wall
with compliments in kind.
Love remains

bridgeably immeasurable.
We are *les certains*
les autres are not,
unmistakably sane –
Santa is our god.
Prayerfully, we forget
les autres really
exist. Beyond concern
they die. One simply
has to think of them.

Reality and Dreams

all characters in God's dreams
direct our perceptions and dreams

nothing matters but dreams
he wouldn't dream of; he did dream

all characters in God's dreams
are real and not real

dreams are insubstantial dreams of God
his own dreams are shadows

he longed in his wish-dream
for dreams, real, frighteningly real

real between dreams and reality
resentful of that dream partly dreamed

the reality from which dream emerged
dream haunts his dreams lost in dreams

that world of dreams and reality
types and shadows, facts and illusions

real, back to reality
I had a dream; I forget my dreams

and Caesar's wife had dreams
she isn't real, no, she's not real

I dreamt in your dream, more of your dream
where dreams are reality and reality is dreams

everything starts from dream
reality and dream

Sister Agnieszka *Is* Carmine Revenge

Stand on that hill, the director says,
like a strawberry scented switchblade,
splayed, you know the kind, propped up
for a retail shot on wegotknives.com.
Spread those legs and stand on that hill
like Modesty Blaise, your hands on your hips.
He keeps pointing, angling his head
but there is no hill,

only a screen of green
from floor to ceiling. He hovers on his crane
as she ascends the scaffold. A novice,
hurled into this business, not from obscurity
but from a life starred with beauty
earned by her vigilant eye, a gift
the Buddhists call Bodhi. On meeting
the director she noticed his hands, dictating

the air round her coif, flat palms slicing,
miming a box for her face – a canvas, blank,
already framed. He pulled out a lipstick,
in three slick swathes painted a mouth
over her mouth. Now she stands –
in a studio just south of Pinewood, her trailer
downwind of the portaloos. Starlet, muse, smile
the colour of rage:

Carmine Revenge.
Her name in the blood of a thousand cochineal:
the tagline would ooze on posters
in moth-gnawed theatres beside saunas
and vape stores. Sister climbs down for a fag break,
swats away the make-up team like gnats.
She considers the girl in the catering van,
her greasepaint, the perfume of tallow. A grace

to her application, dedication to the craft
of flipping, anointing grey burgers
with red snogs of ketchup. A crane fly
sizzles to a hiss on the grill. The director
calls the crew to set, by megaphone. O
He who must be, architect, creator
of this creature feature –
Daddy longlegs.

An Evil Twin

I'll be – when I am dead, or gone –
maligned and, worse, misunderstood,

for half of me can do no wrong,
the other half can do no good:

what fatal motor drives me on
is in the blood, is in the blood.

Lily Blacksell

I want you to know I believe in myself

For all the times she's wondered
what's he thinking what's he thinking

and answered her own question with
of course of course fuck all

admittedly inaccurate yes she knows that
yes she knows that he is thinking

of escaping et voilà hey presto
who'd have guessed before long she is too.

How is it that the hunter's suddenly feeling
ever so hunted. A beast of prey in brown

brown brown with pressure points yes
pressure points doused in uninspiring scent.

To admit he has got under her skin is
a brave salute to cliché. Blood is nothing

new to her such a quantity of blood. A matter a fact
of blotting and letting blotting and letting *Shut up*

and listen she'd told him *don't pray.* Sandwiches
like diamonds are for her at least forever.

He has smoked salmon then lamb cutlets
as often as he can which brings us back

to the format of the one following the other
it is one thing after another in this blood

business together once it gets going
there's no stopping blood. Just like a runaway

disguised as a monk getting into a station wagon
Père Noël at Bon Marché is in no way what he seems.

Listen she said *I caused miracles.* See how the light
changed as she said it see how the clouds zoomed in

the wind see how the Seine is the very same colour
as the sky that hangs above it see how there are shadows

there are doubts.

Comme il Faut

At College Sunrise, everyone
has a washed up story to tell

all inmates of one state or another
and a blank set of careless intentions.

They may be a practised Swiss cook
or like seagulls or hold a plover's egg.

He doesn't smoke the stuff, she's
always in the office with her lists.

No matter, they all want something
priceless and French for their money.

How to romance things like broken legs?
Peer through the mist to the lake shore.

See the ruined families, observe savage
gangs of Scots, the catatonic poses.

The murder of Queen Mary's Lord Darnley
isn't a dream or someone playing a game.

If the crash doesn't happen in his family
if his state of mind is running away with itself

into the pith of a choking and itching
the sensation of a prisoner in a dank dungeon

the least a writer worthy of his hire must do
is write jealousy into a literary profession.

He must take the motorbike for a spin
in the mountains on a cold sunny day

let his mind soar above the clouds as he tries
to recall the few notes of the tune on the violin.

Slowly unwinding into a work of art should be
a far simpler affair than this notebook of manners.

It's so marvellous to learn how to arrange
flowers that aren't there whatever the title.

Matthew Caley

The Fern

I

You begin, by setting your scene –
watch as I heat up some crack
in a blow-torched spoon
with nothing at stake
but the roundness of the moon –
her place held above the lake,
mirror to pallor, its sheen
enclosing her, her wake
and wispy filaments fine
as the spokes on a child's bike
when in full motion.

II

You begin, by setting your scene –
diversions a plot might take:
some super-rich Europeans,
the redoubtable Mdme Spark,
The Prisoner of Chillon,
those who claim writer's block,
their need to be ordained
with sloth, their hides like *Shellac* –
all writhe in this book,
come off Methadone, then turn
again to the dropper's neck.

III

You begin, by setting your scene –
watch as…the child dumps that bike
in dead-beat rhododendrons
by a broken hunter's shack
pausing to rub his tendons.
Earphones act as his wind-brake.
…how this curled, serrated fern
off the wrong path, in deep spring
seems so much more a fern,
an inkling, not a twig-crack
that might make him turn.

Nazia Mohammad, 'here'

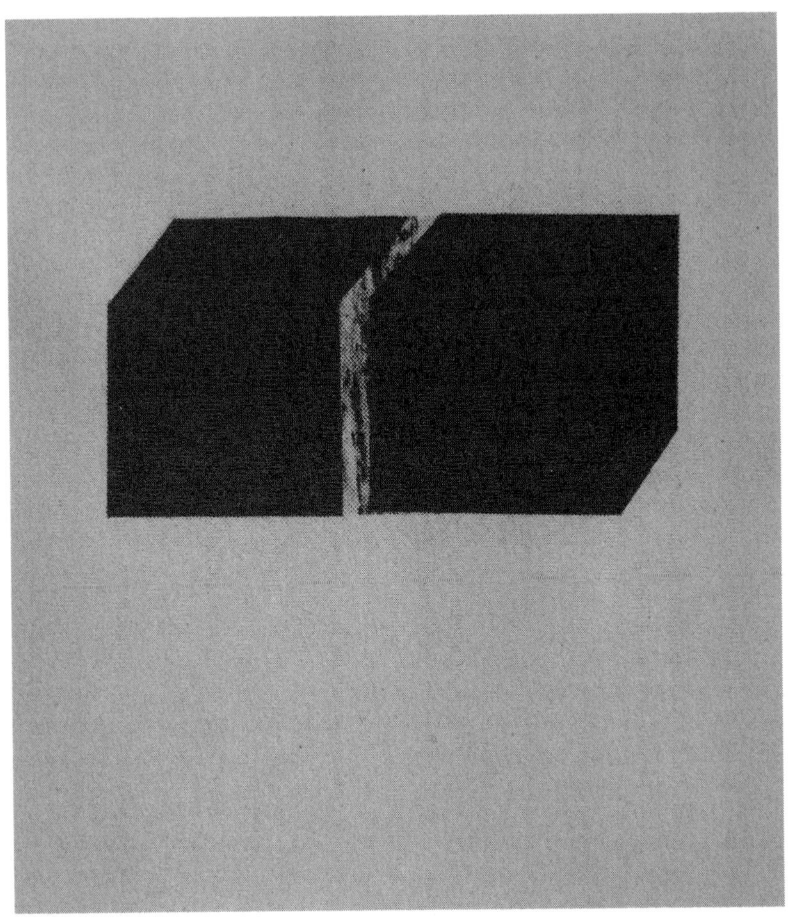

NOTES

Many of the poems contain phrases, echoes and references from their respective novels, used in creative ways, and it would be pointless to list all of those here.

The *Spiritus Sanctus* print was photographed by Alice Smith.

p.19 **Mrs Pettigrew replies:** the majority of words in this poem are taken directly from *Memento Mori* and mixed together with a few additions by the poem's author.
p.23 **The Ballad of Peckham Rye**: the epigraph is from *The Life of William Blake* by Alexander Gilchrist, first published in 1863.
p.32 **Futurist Cleopatra**: in addition to *The Prime of Miss Jean Brodie*, sources for this poem are: William Shakespeare, *Antony and Cleopatra*. F.T. Marinetti, translated by R.W. Flint, *The Futurist Manifesto*. Wikipedia page for Hurricane Debbie (1961), accessed 17.00 on 7 August 2018: https://en.wikipedia.org/wiki/Hurricane_Debbie_(1961).
p.56 **Elsa's Shadow Falls Toward the Sun**: the epigraph is from René Char's poem 'Make it So!'.
p.72 **Letter from Nemi**: the epigraph is from 'Mothers as Makers of Death' by Claudia Dey, *the Paris Review*, 14 August, 2018.
p.75 **Studio Apartment: Eyrie:** the epigraph is from 'How to reach the eyrie', chapter XXXII, *The Art of Falconry, Volume 2*, by Emperor Frederick II of Hohenstaufen, translated by Casey A. Wood, F. Marjorie Fyfe.
p.77 **Sea Flower**: the epigraph is from *Big Sur and the Oranges of Hieronymus Bosch* (1957) by Henry Miller.
p.93 **Reality and Dreams**: this poem contains every mention of the words 'reality' and 'dreams' in the novel.

ACKNOWLEDGEMENTS

Thanks to all the poets and artists for offering their work to this anthology, none of which has been previously published.

We'd also like to thank Olga for her introduction; Gerry for the cover; Ian and Sam for suggesting and designing the Blue Diode logo; Alice and John for the Spiritus Sanctus print.

Thanks to Nancy Somerville for her proof-reading skills and to Helena Nelson for much-needed advice on publishing and book creation.

And, of course, thanks to Muriel for the spark.

BIOGRAPHIES

Juana Adcock is a Mexican-raised, Glasgow-based poet and translator working in English and Spanish.

Polly Atkin lives in Cumbria. Her first collection *Basic Nest Architecture* (Seren: 2017) is followed by a third pamphlet, *With Invisible Rain* (New Walk Press: 2018).

Deborah Alma is editor of three poetry anthologies, her first poetry collection *Dirty Laundry* is with Nine Arches Press. She is Emergency Poet prescribing poetry from her vintage ambulance and teaches at Keele University.

Janette Ayachi (b. 1982) is a Scottish-Algerian poet and her first full poetry collection *Hand Over Mouth Music* will be released by Liverpool University Press in early 2019.

Simon Barraclough is a poet, writer and performer. *Los Alamos Mon Amour* (Salt 2008), *Bonjour Tetris* (Penned in the Margins 2010), *Neptune Blue* (Salt 2011), *Sunspots* (Penned in the Margins 2015).

Paul Batchelor was born in Northumberland. He teaches English Literature and Creative Writing at Durham University. His publications include *The Sinking Road* (Bloodaxe, 2008) and *The Love Darg* (Clutag, 2014).

Dzifa Benson is a multi-disciplinary live artist who uses literature as her primary mode of expression. She is currently studying for an MA in Text & Performance at Birkbeck and RADA.

Sarah Bernstein is a writer from Montreal. Her work has appeared in *tender, Cumulus, Adjacent Pineapple, Contemporary Women's Writing, Room Magazine* etc. Her first book, *Now Comes the Lightning*, was published in Canada by Pedlar Press in 2015.

Tessa Berring lives in Edinburgh. Recent poetry can be found via Pitymilk Press (*DUETDUET*), Dancing Girl Press (*Cut Glass and No Flowers*), *Datableedzine, A) Glimpse) Of)*, and *Adjacent Pineapple.*

Lily Blacksell's pamphlet *There's No Such Thing* is published by ignitionpress. She has an MFA in poetry from Columbia University, where she was also a teaching fellow. She lives in London.

Jane Bonnyman is from Edinburgh. Her first pamphlet, *An Ember from the Fire: Poems on the Life of Fanny Van de Grift Stevenson*, was published by Poetry Salzburg in 2016.

Zoë Brigley Thompson is Assistant Professor at the Ohio State University. She has two poetry collections *The Secret* (2007) and *Conquest* (2012). Her third collection and her nonfiction essays are forthcoming in 2019. Zoebrigley.com

Judy Brown's *Crowd Sensations* (Seren, 2016) was shortlisted for the Ledbury Forte Prize. Her first book, *Loudness* (Seren, 2011), was shortlisted for the Forward first collection prize. judy-brown.co.uk

Larry Butler teaches tai-chi and leads expressive writing groups at the Maggie Cancer Care Centre. Poet & editor for PlaySpace Publications and for Lapidus Scotland: http://wordsworkwellscotland.co.uk/

Matthew Caley's most recent and 5th collection is *Rake* (Bloodaxe, 2016). He's been a tutor for The Poetry School and is Associate Lecturer in Contemporary Poetry / Creative Writing at St Andrew's University. He lives in London.

Vahni Capildeo's most recent book is *Venus as a Bear* (Carcanet, 2018). Capildeo lives in Edinburgh, and is the Douglas Caster Cultural Fellow in Poetry at the University of Leeds.

Rishi Dastidar is a member of Malika's Poetry Kitchen. His debut collection is *Ticker-tape* (Nine Arches Press, 2017); a poem from it was included in The Forward Book of Poetry 2018.

Tishani Doshi publishes poetry, fiction and essays. Her most recent book is *Girls are Coming out of the Woods* (Bloodaxe Books, 2018).

Sasha Dugdale is a poet and translator. Her fourth collection *Joy* was a PBS Choice in 2017 and the title poem won the Forward Prize for Best Single Poem in 2016.

Matthew Francis is the author of six poetry collections, most recently his adaptation of *The Mabinogi*. His edition of W.S. Graham's *New Selected Poems* was published in September 2018.

M.G. Garland travels often to the Holy Land for purposes of religious and archaeological research, and attends to chickens, poems, incomplete knots and unusual plants in a Midlands village.

Natalie Gale is an artist who works and lives in Durham, currently an Academic Tutor at The University of Sunderland. She studied at the Slade University College, London, and Wimbledon School of Art.

W.N. Herbert is a Professor of Poetry & Creative Writing at Newcastle University. His most recent collection is *Omnesia* (Bloodaxe, 2013). In September 2013, he was appointed as Dundee's first makar.

Colin Herd is a poet and Lecturer in Creative Writing at University of Glasgow. His books include *Too Ok* (BlazeVox, 2011), *Glovebox* (Knives, Forks and Spoons, 2014), *Click and Collect* (Boiler House Press, 2017) and *Swamp Kiss* (Red Ceilings Press, 2018). www.colinherd.com

Andy Jackson's most recent poetry collection is *A Beginner's Guide To Cheating* (Red Squirrel 2015). He has edited several anthologies including *Split Screen, Double Bill* and *Whaleback City* (with W.N. Herbert). A new anthology *Scotia Extremis* (co-edited with Brian Johnstone) is due in late 2018 from Luath Press.

Robert Alan Jamieson is a poet and novelist, originally from Shetland. He has tutored Creative Writing at the University of Edinburgh for the last twenty years.

Lisa Kelly is Chair of Magma Poetry. Her debut collection, *A Map Towards Fluency* is forthcoming from Carcanet, June 2019.

Frances Leviston has published two collections of poetry, *Public Dream* (2007) and *Disinformation* (2015), both with Picador. She teaches creative writing at the University of Manchester.

Joanne Limburg's latest poetry collection is *The Autistic Alice* (Bloodaxe, 2017). She is a Lecturer in Creative Writing at De Montfort University.

Gerry Loose is a poet. As well as his print publications, his poetry can to be found in Botanic Gardens, hospitals, natural spaces and galleries.

Jeanette Lynes directs the MFA in Writing at University of Saskatchewan, Canada. Her latest poetry collection is *Bedlam Cowslip: The John Clare Poems.* Her second novel is *The Small Things That End The World.*

Rachael Macarthur (b.1981, Edinburgh) is an artist interested in the difficulties of translating memory through the difficulties of a painting process. Her practice includes painting, drawing, installation and ceramics.

Rob A. Mackenzie's most recent poetry collection is *The Good News* (Salt, 2013). He co-organises a monthly Edinburgh live poetry event, *Vespers*, and is reviews editor of *Magma Poetry* magazine.

Iain Matheson was born in Plean. He is a long-time musician and more recent poet. His poems are included in *Umbrellas of Edinburgh* and *House of Three, Season 2 Volume 4.*

Drew Milne's collected poems, *In Darkest Capital*, were published by Carcanet in 2017. *Earthworks* is forthcoming from Equipage. *Third Nature* is forthcoming from Dostoevsky Wannabe.

Nazia Mohammad is an artist based in Edinburgh exploring themes of grief, mysticism and spiritual practises using a minimalist approach with sculpture, print and film.

Spark's Edinburgh is occasionally recognisable in the one **Iain Morrison** lives in. His collection *I'm A Pretty Circler* comes out with Vagabond Voices in autumn 2018. permanentpositions. wordpress.com

Helena Nelson is the editor/originator of HappenStance Press, which specialises in poetry pamphlets. She also writes poems.

Sean O'Brien's ninth poetry collection is *Europa* (2018). He is a Professor of Creative Writing at Newcastle University and a Fellow of the Royal Society of Literature.

Louise Peterkin's poems have featured in publications including *Magma, The Dark Horse* and *The North*. In 2016 she won a New Writers Award for poetry from the Scottish Book Trust.

Richard Price's books: *The Island, Lucky Day* and *Small World* (file under fathers and daughters, and daughters and fathers). *Moon for Sale* was a Guardian Poetry Book of the Year.

Eileen Pun is a poet, diarist, farmer and martial artist and has received awards for her interdisciplinary work. She is published internationally and has edited several books on Chinese culture and philosophy.

Anna Selby is a poet and naturalist. Her poetry often explores our connection with water and the natural world. She aims for her poems to share a sense of compassion and attentiveness to the environment.

James Sheard is the author of three collections with Cape. He lives in the Welsh Marches with the poet Deborah Alma and lectures at Keele University.

Lindsey Shields Waters lives in Glasgow. She was a Clydebuilt 10 mentee for 2016/17 and her poems have featured in various magazines and anthologies including *Magma, Gutter and Lighthouse.*

Lisa Smithey's work in ceramics aims to elevate the seemingly mundane details of daily life through abstracted forms. These works may arise from objects encountered in her own life or from classic literary narratives.

Tim Turnbull's latest poetry collection, *Avanti!* is available from Red Squirrel Press. He lives in highland Perthshire, where he teaches, paints, and is currently working on a novel and a collection of short stories.

Tony Williams's poetry publications include *The Midlands* and *The Corner of Arundel Lane & Charles Street*. He lives in Northumberland and works in Newcastle-upon-Tyne.

Olga Wojtas attended James Gillespie's High School, immortalised as Marcia Blaine School in *The Prime of Miss Jean Brodie*. Olga's debut novel is *Miss Blaine's Prefect and the Golden Samovar.*